AGNOSTIC CRITIQUE
of
THE BIBLE

RAYMOND A. HULT

Order this book online at www.trafford.com
or email orders@trafford.com

Most Trafford titles are also available at major online book retailers.

Print information available on the last page.

ISBN: 978-1-6987-1287-1 (sc)
ISBN: 978-1-6987-1288-8 (e)

Scripture quotations marked KJV are from the Holy Bible, King James
Version (Authorized Version). First published in 1611. Quoted from the KJV
Classic Reference Bible, Copyright © 1983 by The Zondervan Corporation.

Trafford rev. 09/15/2022

 www.trafford.com

North America & international
toll-free: 844-688-6899 (USA & Canada)
fax: 812 355 4082

CONTENTS

PREFACE

Having lived the majority of my 78 years of life as a devout Christian, I never, during that time, questioned the Bible as representing the infallible word of God. Having that assurance, based on continual indoctrination from the time I was born, the thought of questioning anything contained in the Bible never crossed my mind.

Although I had probably read less than 20% of the Bible's content, my impregnatable faith in its divine providence precluded any necessity for evaluating its accuracy and the irrefutable truth it represented.

It wasn't until I retired as an FBI Special Agent in 1998 that I found sufficient time to try to disprove critics of Christianity. Instead, I discovered a few areas of concern that I found difficult to refute. That morphed over the next few years into more and more of the same; until finally, I was able to reverse the mind control that had consumed my life and admit, for the fits time; I was unsure what represented the truth and what didn't.

I was finally able to reasonably analyze biblical content. What I discovered was I had been committed to scripture that no longer made sense and couldn't be proven beyond a shadow of doubt. My opinion of what the Bible had to say didn't hold up to careful scrutiny of what it represented to be the truth.

I'm now more prone to believe the Bible embodies the fabrication of mere humans for whatever motives they may have had for its creation. No real God would have anything to do with authorizing such a defective and improbable collection of verses.

This book doesn't come close to addressing all the problems I see with biblical content. It tackles many of the most significant ones. Hopefully, that's sufficient to impress upon the reader the Bible falling short of credibly establishing its substance.

ONE

QUESTIONING THE EXISTENCE OF GOD

Although seeming nonsensical in this day and age, many inhabitants in ancient Greece believed, without reservation, in the existent of Greek gods.

Initially, the first divine entity was Eros, the god of love and procreation. Following was a myriad of additional gods including Qurea, the god of the mountains, Pontus, the god of the sea, Uranus, the god of the heavens etc. etc.

Although religious supporters today consider the Greek gods to have been the invented figments of over-active imaginations, I have to wonder why there's no similar skepticism concerning their God as portrayed in the Bible. Should there be?

Differences of opinion between Agnostics like myself and devout biblical advocates proliferate, to say the least. A question I frequently bring up often stops committed adherents in their tracks. Where did your God come from? If unable to answer that, how is it possible to know for sure such a divine being actually exists and isn't a mere fabrication of your imagination?

The biblical God is described as being omnipotent, omniscient, omnipresent and omnibenevolent; in other words, being perfect and all-powerful in every conceivable way. How did a God exhibiting that degree of amazing complexity and extraordinary capability arrive on the scene?

All of a sudden, appearing out of thin air makes no sense. So, there would have to be some kind of alternative credible explanation to prove such a being subsists in reality.

One interesting response I got was being the offspring of another God with similar attributes. That doesn't solve the dilemma. There can be God's infinitum, but there's no satisfactory explanation until a reasonable enlightenment for the first one can be determined. It's the same conundrum.

The Bible is filled with page after page talking about the power of God, but zero about how He came to be. I would expect that to have been the first subject matter to be revealed in the book of Genesis. It wasn't addressed then and has never been since.

It's difficult justifying the worship of an extra-terrestrial deity whose origin is impossible to establish. And if that's the unsolvable puzzle, the biblical God more reasonably might be labeled an incompressible entity having little more plausibility of actual existence than the Greek gods.

I'm more of an Agnostic than an Atheist. An Atheist is normally considered to be a person who maintains there's no God—period! An Agnostic, on the other hand, believes nothing about the existence of God can be known beyond a shadow of a doubt, one way or the other. What I'm more confident about is there's never been any connection made between any godly being and humans.

How did the earth and human life originate? I don't know for sure. There're basically two concepts argued between organized religious believers and those who rely on the scientific hypothesis. Believers, in large part, rely on a godly creator as set forth in the Bible. Non-believers support the "big-bang" theory.

Considering the scientific theory of the "big bang," the alleged explosion is almost incomprehensible. A nuclear explosion is massive. An originating bang is trillions of times that massive and still exploding. It has been estimated the current distance from earth to the present edge of the Universe is about 46.6 billion light-years away. Unfathomable!

Scientific explanations of how life started on earth include: (1) Lightning generating amino acids and sugar from the atmosphere loaded with water, methane, ammonia and hydrogen. (2) Deep sea submarine hydrothermal vents spewing elements key to life like carbon and hydrogen. That starts the theory of evolution from microscopic life forms to present-day humanity.

As unfathomable as it appears, I have to favor the scientific explanation of how earthly life started over the explanation in Genesis for one indisputable reason. There's simply no existing plausible explanation for the origin of a biblical creator.

TWO

GENESIS (THE CREATION)

How did Moses obtain the information concerning the creation? No one knows for sure the source allowing him to compile the First Book of Moses called Genesis. There are various theories, but nothing for sure.

Many religious theorists believe that knowledge was passed down to him through an oral history of hearsay from Adam. It is believed Adam would have been subject to first-hand information, having been there at the beginning. Nothing in the Bible to verify this unlikely supposition.

Because humans back then are alleged to have experienced extremely long-life spans (also unlikely), it theoretically may not have taken that long a list of people to pass along that knowledge; Some theorize it being passed along from Adam to Lamech to Shem to Abraham.

From that point, it's theorized it might have required only the addition of as few as four more generations until Moses was informed while leading the Israelites in the desert. Who knows? Nobody for sure. One thing I contend is there's a lot in any such theoretical account that makes me question its authenticity.

I personally find it difficult to accept the genuineness of the Genesis account when the source of the information (Moses) isn't conclusively pinned down That requires in somehow proving the details actually originated with God or someone who assisted him; someone privy to all stages of the creation as set forth in Genesis.

That's probably the investigator in me from my past employment as an FBI Special Agent. That's the kind of evidence I would have required in order to not have it thrown out of court based the unreliable nature of hearsay proof. Although I can't verify for certain the account attributed to Moses was entirely bogus, it raises my level of suspicion for sure.

The progression of the creative detail provided also troubles me. Moses records that God created light on the first day, but didn't get around to creating the sun and the moon until the fourth day. What was the source of light for the first 3 days?

If the sun wasn't created until the fourth day, what was the earth rotating around, since it was reportedly created on the first. Wouldn't it have soared far out into the Universe without the gravitational pull of the sun?

Genesis depicts God created grass, herbs and fruit bearing trees on the third day. But, again, there was no sun until the fourth. I guess a God could create plant life without sun or heat, but it seems odd to me.

Genesis specifies Heaven was created on the 2nd day. Where was God living if it wasn't in Heaven?

Things equally difficult for me to readily accept are set forth in chapter 2 concerning Adam and Eve. It indicates Adam was created first from the dust and Eve thereafter from one of Adam's ribs. Why would there be a difference in the method? Truthfully, it makes no sense to me how dust or a rib would be used as the source of the human body.

It goes on to explain that Satan, disguised as a talking snake, beguiled Eve into eating the forbidden fruit. God then placed a curse on Satan and cast both Adam and Eve out of the garden. This was the origin of the concept of "original sin" requiring the ultimate sacrifice of Jesus to erase it and allow humans to inherit a heavenly abode.

Why label all humans sinful from the get-go when the only ones that did anything sinful were Adam and Eve? Doesn't seem fair to me. It appears upon reflection to be an unnecessary two-event plan having nothing to do with how the rest of humanity obeyed or disobeyed God's commandments.

I apologize if I appear rude, but to be honest, most of the account of Genesis reminds me of Greek mythology passed down from generation to generation. Plausible and enticing to some, but lacking believability by those like myself.

THREE

THE UNIVERSE

The First Book of Mosses Called Genesis is referred to as proving the Universe ("firmament") was created by God on the second day of his creative process. As an Agnostic, I have my doubts that actually happened. I can't prove it didn't, but I also see no credible proof it did. I'd say about a 99% chance no such godly creative effort ever took place.

Wondering specifically what believers rely upon to justify such a massive undertaking, I researched some scriptures in the Bible and ask around. A few of the justifications I came up with included the following:

1. "The heavens disclose the glory of God; and the firmament sheweth his handy work" (Psalm 19:1)
2. "As the heaven is high above the earth, so great is his mercy toward them that fear him" (Psalm 103:11)

3. The Universe manifests the glory of God. It provides a perspective of the power of God as compared to the limited capability of mere mortals. It humbles humanity into worshiping the enormous capability of their creator.

4. God intends to let the redeemed one day explore the rest of the Universe. With the length of time that eternity affords, it makes sense that a vast Universe would be required.

5. The Universe may contain multi-millions of inhabited planets just like Earth. Therefore, the immensity of it may not be all that huge when all such planets are considered.

Considering a few of the unfathomable statistics scientists have postulated, the known Universe contains well over 100 billion galaxies with an estimated total of roughly 10 billion trillion stars. Our Sun is just one of those stars. The Universe is still expanding at an unimaginable rate. Estimates have it continuing to increase at the volumetric rate of a trillion cubic light-years (the distance it takes light to travel in a year-cubed) with no end in sight.

The Andromeda Galaxy (just one of the 100 billion) is closest to the Milky Way Galaxy of which our Earth occupies a relatively minuscule speck of space. If the distance between the two galaxies was reduced (for comparative purposes only) to the distance between someone's eyes and a book being read, the most remote galaxy of which we are aware would currently be nearly 1.2 miles away.

Concerning 1 and 2 above, there's no concrete proof the opinions set forth in Psalm are the result in anything more than the speculation of a human most likely speciously representing the creative planning of a divine being; an unrealistic conjecture at best.

Responses from unnamed persons in 3-5 are likewise attempts to offer explanations likewise based on conjecture with absolutely no back-up proof of any kind. For example, the idea of there being countless other planets inhabited by mortals like us is mere unsubstantiated guesswork at present.

So, now we come to the more obvious rationalization having to do with common sense. Why would God feel it necessary to create something so massive? There're enough stars and rotating planets around them in the Milky Way alone to display the glory, power and creative intent of any God. What would be the purpose of such a gargantuan expansion continuing today and far into the foreseeable future?

The only logical conclusion is the Universe has evolved by some other means than as part of some divinely-concocted plan to complement the Earth.

FOUR

INTELLIGENT DESIGN?

For those biblical devotees who agitate against the theory of evolution and contend the complexity of the human body proves the necessity of a master designer, I have to wonder if that supposedly godly-inspired blueprint of bodily design is all it's cracked up to be.

Admittedly, the physical structure of human beings is amazing in the intricacy of its component parts. The anatomical construction of the human eye is just one example arguing for something more than the creation of human beings evolving from the continuous mutation of DNA combined with the survival of the fittest over billions of years.

Nevertheless, doubt remains in contending to the contrary. How do you explain the imperfect aspects of the human anatomy, while still attributing it to an allegedly perfect and faultless creator?

Newborns are continuously dying due to imperfections in the human structure. If not dying, all kinds of genetic defects cause untold anguish leading to lives loaded with grueling challenges that often result in leading a less than idyllic life experience. Or, perhaps, does it make more sense to impute such deficiencies to cellular disfunction due to the normal evolutionary process?

A significant percentage of earth's population, at any one time, suffers from a myriad of incapacitating ailments. I have to wonder why, for example, the God of the Bible couldn't have done a better job in making us more resistant to the magnitude of incapacitating afflictions. Why did He create the immune response of some so much more effective than that of others?

I don't see much intelligent design in creating an immune system uncapable of repelling the various viruses and bacteria incessantly invading our bodies. Some suffer from cancer and other such debilitating afflictions while others escape risk free. What kind of faultless system of uniformly creative design is that?

Remarkable as the human body is, the crucial feature making it superior to the rest of the animal world is the superior function of its brain. Other than that, we're not all that impressive in many instances when compared to other allegedly inferior species.

Alligators, for example, have a thick hide protecting them to a far greater extent than the flimsy covering provided by human skin. The fact is, without the superior capability of the human brain, our species of Homo Sapiens would have most likely become extinct by now having lost the battle to successfully compete with far more hardy animal varieties.

The five senses of human are amazing, but obviously inferior when measured against the capability of other lesser endowed species. The eyes of birds of prey are superior in observing in great detail their quarry at far greater distance than the inferior capability of the human eye.

If the biblical God intelligently created humans, it would seem logical to expect, in addition to our brain, that all our other critical body parts and senses would have been perfectly designed as well; certainly, when compared to that of lesser species. That's simply not the case.

Assuming a divine creator intended the human race to be the superior species, it would seem logical He wouldn't have stopped at the brain. He would have included smell superior to that of the African elephant with the number of genes (around 2,000) associated with the sense of smell; around five times as many as humans.

Superior to the taste of the catfish with more than 175,000 taste sensitive cells compared to the average humane with only 100,000.

Dogs can hear a lot of high frequencies humans are incapable of. They can normally hear up to 45 kHz compared to just 20 kHz in the human high hearing range.

Doesn't evolution seem more logical, than any godly creation, when rationalizing the positive and negative attributes of living organisms? Isn't it more likely it's been the continual genetic mutation of DNA that best explains the non-intelligent specie's superior diversity?

FIVE

HUMAN SUFFERING

How do those faithful, accepting of the Bible as reflecting the will of their God, explain the immense suffering by the human race since the beginning of recorded history? War, crime, natural disaster, sickness, poverty, and persecution are examples of the agony that has caused horrendous human distress that never seems to abate.

Just a few examples include the genocide of over 6 million innocent Jews by the Nazis, the early 1900s worldwide flu pandemic that killed millions more innocent victims, and the 2010 earthquake in Haiti estimated to have wiped out over 200 thousand inhabitants with millions more suffering the almost total destruction of its largest city.

If God is absolutely powerful and compassionate, how can believers explain his apparent willingness to allow, or his inability to stop, the never-ending torment that continues to permeate our earthly existence on such a massive scale? For those Christians, Jews and Muslims who accept accounts of the Old Testament as reflecting reality, there can be no question their God has unlimited capabilities involving the total control of what happens in mortality. The Bible clearly infers that its God could eliminate human suffering if He chose to do so.

The God of the Bible displayed this capability when he saved the Israelites from death and suffering by stopping the advance of the attacking Egyptian army across the Red Sea. For those who believe that the Book of Exodus reflects an actual account of events, it is apparent the biblical God is also capable of selectively stopping those who may cause suffering without harming the innocent in the process.

For example, in chapter 9 of Exodus, God is reported as selectively destroying the food source (cattle) of the Egyptians but not of the Israelites; causing medical afflictions (boils and blains) on the Egyptians, but not the Israelites; and sending hail and fire upon the Egyptians without harming his chosen people.

The Bible makes it clear that even Jesus Christ, in his somewhat limited role on earth, as part God-part human, was capable of redirecting the forces of nature, healing the terminally ill, and even causing the dead to rise again. Why then would a God with the obvious power to eliminate the unconscionable anguish of billions of innocent humans purposely decide to allow it to occur?

Among the explanations, unproven and not outlined in the Bible, for the suffering, a couple of the most frequent possible justifications I've encountered include: (1) Suffering is a necessary component of mortality as a test of faith in times of distress and disaster, (2) It's God's way of punish those who disobey him, (3) The only way to appreciate what eternal life has to offer is to experience what it's like without it, and (4) Humans are currently incapable of understanding the necessity of suffering. Sometime, in the distant future, that reason will be made obvious.

Explanations 1-3 suffer from the obvious reality that suffering isn't equally applied. As a test, some suffer way more than others. Some barely suffer at all. What sense does a test make if a large segment of humanity is barely tested at all.

Concerning punishment, the biblical record is clear that the innocent, including blameless women and guiltless children, were made to suffer in addition to the alleged guilty. What kind of divinely instituted response is that?

If suffering is intended to be a necessary component in appreciating what it will be like without it, again, how about all those humans who experience it at far lesser degree or not at all do to early demise. What kind of appreciation does that entail for those who barely have a chance to experience it.

Regarding rationalization #4, there's no way to know for sure if that represents a credible response or simply a convenient cop-out that begs the question. However, I can't imagine a legitimate and caring biblical God who would limit comment on such a critical subject involving the well-being of the human race, while often going into great detail regarding biblical matters of far less significance.

Logic tells me that the Bible is more likely a concoction of the human mind and has nothing to do with an actual supreme being or divine designer. If such a God does exist, such a being is either unwilling or incapable of impacting the suffering of earthlings who more logically appear to be solely responsible, along with the independent whims of Mother Nature (unguided by any godly force), for our own state of human discomfort and grief.

If incapable, then the Bible is suspect in all it represents because the God of the Bible is represented as being fully capable of doing anything He so desires. If capable, but unwilling, that's not the kind of God I could respect or worship. Until someone can show me a humane and plausible explanation for purposely allowing the incomprehensible suffering that occurs on such a massive scale, I'm inclined at present to side with those who reject the credibility of the Bible.

SIX

ANGELS

The Bible is chockfull of accounts involving angels. Descriptions include the following:

- Angels are spiritual beings (Psalm 104:4, Hebrews 1:14).
- They inhabit the spiritual realm called heaven (Mark 13:32, Galatians 1:8).
- They can be in only one place at a time (Daniel 10:11-14).
- They are immortal. They were created at one point in time, but they don't die (Luke 20:36).
- They don't marry (Matthew 22:30).

Their missions as recorded in the Bible are numerous and varied. Their tasks include acting as sentinels for God, killing evil doers, protecting believers and passing on various messages on behalf of God. The powers attributed to angels are immense. For example, in 2 Kings 19: 35, an angel is reported to have slain 185,000 Assyrians in the course of a single night.

The description of angels by Ezekiel and Isaiah discloses some having multiple faces and wings. The faces include features of animals. They are often seen wearing long white ankle-length robes covering their spirit-like forms. They can apparently communicate through words that are understandable to humans.

Angels are mentioned **as** appearing 273 times in the Bible. There's no credible evidence of them appearing once today. Some may claim they have, but we have nothing but their word to prove it. Why is that? With the world-wide internet, it would take only one such appearance of an incontestable extra-terrestrial angelic being to validate the reality of their existence.

I don't think I'm beings unreasonable when questioning the reality of multiple animal faces and sets of wings as part of the physical makeup of angels. To me, that's more like the description of fictitious characters in a fairy tale.

Surely God, if one exists, wouldn't expect me to rely entirely on the Bible for proof of angelic interactions with humans. With narratives occurring so long ago, it's now impossible to verify them today. Proof requires something more than somebody simply claiming something happened.

Could it be because angels never existed in the first place? Going back far enough means not being burdened with proving their reality now. Faith is all that is required.

SEVEN

FOUR GOSPELS

The Four Gospels (Gos) in the Bible allegedly contain The Gospel According to Matthew, Mark, Luke and John. They form the bedrock of the New Testament. They're the four books recording almost everything we know about Jesus. If readers can't trust these ancient texts as representing a true account of the life and accomplishments of Jesus, confidence in the remainder of the New Testament becomes similarly tainted.

My agnostic inclination is not to accept the truthfulness of the Gos accounts simply because they're part of the Bible. It takes logic and credible evidence to convince me; neither of which exist. There are two significant arguments why that's the case.

The first problem that stands out is that all four books are compiled in the third person. Although readers may assume all four writers were part of the original twelve apostles, in the constant presence of Jesus with first-hand knowledge of his accomplishments, there's good reason to suspect that wasn't the case.

Experts estimate the Gos were penned decades after Jesus died. Most estimate date somewhere around 70 AD for Mark, 80-90 AD for Mathew and Luke, and 95 AD for John. Assuming members of the twelve were about the same age as Jesus, they would have been between 70 and 95 years old: most likely too old to have authored the Gos. Especially, when considering the life expectancy of men at that time was considerably less.

That suggests the Gos weren't according to any of the twelve apostles. They were by someone representing themselves to be the same. It indicates the veracity of the content would be severely downgraded as a result of multiple layers of unreliable hearsay.

The second problem is even more problematic due to the conflicting accounts of the authors of all four books. They simply got their hearsay mixed up and reported alleged similar events significantly different from each other.

Although there are many more inconsistencies, I'll cover those surrounding the death and resurrection of Jesus to make the point. I suggest readers compare all four books to obtain a full accounting of all the numerous additional contradictions.

The Four Gos writers report dissimilar accounts of those who first approached the empty tomb of Christ. Matthew reports it was Mary Magdalene and "the other Mary" -not identified (Matthew 28:1). Mark identifies the persons as "Mary Magdalene, and Mary, the mother of James and Salome" (Mark 16:1). Luke says it was it was "Mary Magdalene, and Joanna, and Mary the mother of James, and other women who were with them." (Luke 20:10). John says it was Mary Magdalene and no one else (John 20:1").

The four writers provide differing details when it comes to what happened during the initial approach to the tomb. Matthew says the two Marys were greeted by an angel who descended from heaven following a "great earthquake." (Mat. 28:2-5). Mark says the two Marys and Salome were met by one man sitting inside dressed in a "long white garment." (Mark 16:5). Luke reports the two Marys, Joanna, and the other women were greeted by two men in shining garments standing inside the sepulcher. (Luke 24:4). John says Mary Magdalene alone found the sepulcher empty and wasn't met by anyone. (John 201-2).

There's a difference between the accounts of Matthew and John (Mark and Luke don't comment) as to the setting where the resurrected Jesus allegedly first revealed himself to Mary Magdalene. Matthew says it was to Mary Magdalene and "the other Mary" after they left the sepulcher (Mat 28:8-9). John claims it was to the weeping Mary Magdalene by herself inside the sepulcher (John 20:14-17).

My experience as an FBI Special Agent involved interviewing multiple witnesses simultaneously and separately to help ensure that one's recollection wasn't tainted by the others and to determine the. truth. Contradictions usually meant none could be relied upon to establish the veracity.

It smells to me that whoever was falsely attributing the Gos to the original apostles were likewise unable to establish credible accounts due to the unreliable nature of information based on decades old hearsay. That and the possibility the writers (whoever they were) were swayed to create, for the purpose of establishing a new religious following, fictitious accounts involving the life and miraculous chronicles related to Jesus.

EIGHT

VIRGIN BIRTH?

Part of my philosophy as a committed Agnostic involves depending more on science than miracles. That doesn't mean I exclude the possibility miracles have occurred; just, that I'm going to require additional collaborative proof one has transpired. Simply depending on unprovable faith isn't sufficient.

The problem with the claim of a virgin birth is it falls short of convincing me it ever happened. Joseph and Mary could have been lying for any number of reasons. A supposed miracle could have been later invented as part of a strategy to encourage non-believers to become Christians. Who knows exactly what other viable motives may have been involved?

Call me a raving skeptic incapable of accepting the possibility of a miracle happening. I find it impossible to accept the formation of a human in the womb of a women without the presence of the sperm of a male. That just makes no sense to me at all. There better be more to the claim than just declaring it happened.

Just because the virgin birth is reported in the biblical accounts of St. Mathew and St. Luke doesn't prove it actually transpired. How could either know for sure? The only ones who could would be Joseph and Mary.

Events surrounding the birth as reported by Matthew and Luke appear to contradict each other. Matthew reports three wise men being led by a miraculous star, shepherds being serenaded by a multitude of heavenly hosts, and fleeing to Egypt due to an angelic warning. Luke indicates the family of three simply returning to Nazareth immediately following the birth.

As noted in chapter 7, it's unlikely that the two named apostles related contemporary accounts of Mary's virginity. Most experts believe both gospels were penned decades after the death of Jesus; by writers falsely attributing Matthew and Luke as the authors.

Concerning the attempts by Paul and/or his subsequent followers to expand his new-founded Christian faith, it wouldn't be surprising they might want to stress the idea of a miraculous virgin birth to attract potential converts already accustomed to and many even prone to accepting belief in pagan gods.

Posted on December 8, 2016 by Garrett S. Griffin under Religion, is a discussion of the following pagan gods allegedly born to virgins prior to Mary.

1. Buddha was born of the virgin Maya after the Holy Ghost descended upon her.
2. In Phrgia, Attis was born of the virgin Nama.
3. A Roman Quirrnus was born from a virgin.

4. The Greek deity Adonis was born of the virgin Myrrha, many centuries before the birth of Jesus. He was born "at Bethlehem in the same sacred cave that Christians later claimed as the birthplace of Jesus."

5. In Tibet, Indra was born of a virgin. He ascended into heaven after his death.

6. In Persia, the god Mithra was born of a virgin on Dec. 25th.

7. Also in Persia, Zoroaster was born of a virgin.

8. In India, one of the stories about the birth of Krishna has him being born to his mother Devaki while she was a virgin.

Another source of identifying even more such incidences of virgin births, also pre-dating the birth of Jesus, is contained in the book by John Keyer entitled, *The Ancient Beginnings of the Virgin Birth.*

Adding together all the doubts heretofore mentioned, my Agnostic proclivity must respectively conclude the claim of Jesus having been conceived through the miraculous process of a virgin birth is not only not credibly corroborated, but rationally improbable.

NINE

WERE TEACHINGS OF JESUS UNIQUE?

As an Agnostic, I admire and try to emulate much of the wise counsel attributed to Jesus in the New Testament. The question I have is whether he originated the teachings, or was he just repeating the same kind of ethical imperatives having been propounded by caring human beings during previous recorded history.

Were the lessons Jesus taught truly unique, or did he package, in an admittedly persuasive manner, the same kind of moral priorities the vast majority of us have been inherently wired to comprehend without the necessity of it being taught to us by a godly being; namely, Jesus.

Was it absolutely necessary Jesus instruct us concerning the benefit of abiding by the golden rule? Don't get me wrong. Emphasizing good counsel is beneficial in its own right. What I'm wondering is whether humans never would have grasped the significance unless relayed to us by a divine teacher. Does it prove only a uniquely godlike personage like Jesus could have come up with such sage advice? Otherwise, would we have remained corrupted and in the dark?

Doing a little research, I discovered some previous similar advice about responding to hatred with love. Taoist wisdom, expounded centuries before Jesus was born, warned: "Return love for hatred. Otherwise, when a great hatred is reconciled, some of it will surely remain. How can this end in goodness?"

Buddhist wisdom prior to Jesus counseled: "Shame on him who strikes, greater shame on him who strikes back. Let us live happily, not hating those who hate us."

From ancient Babylonian civilization came the following admonition: "Do not return evil to your adversary: Requite with kindness the one who does evil to you."

The first eleven verses of John mention a women caught in the act of adultery. Jesus cautioned: "Let him who is without sin among you be the first to throw a stone at her."

Not unlike the prior Roman Philosopher, Seneca, who likewise cautioned: "Let him reflect how many times he offends against morality, how many of his acts stand in need of pardon; then he will be angry with himself also. For no just judge pronounce one sort of judgment in his own case a different one in the case of others."

Suffice it to say, we could find similar prior warnings in just about all of the instances when Jesus expounded moral guidance. That didn't make him uniquely godly. It simply proved he was a devout and caring Jew; not unlike many morally- inclined human leaders preceding him.

Any claim, the biblical teachings of Jesus represented unique moral guidance, ignores reality. Most such admonitions previously existed without the additional imperative of divine involvement.

TEN

MIRACLES

It's been estimated the population of Jerusalem, during the life of Jesus, was about 25 thousand. The estimate of the world population in 2021 was closing in on about 7.9 billion. That's about 320 thousand times more humans capable of experiencing a miracle.

There's little doubt I would be an Agnostic if I lived when Jesus did and witnessed the miracles he performed as recorded in the New Testament. Or, possibly, if first-hand witnesses I unequivocally trusted had personally witnessed the same.

There are 37 instances of recorded miracles by Jesus in the Bible, including the following sample of some of the most spectacular: (1) raising of Lazarus and Jairus' daughter from the dead (2) walking on water (3) turning water into wine and (4) healing a blind man.

Truth be told, if I personally witnessed even one of the 37 and was convinced it wasn't the result of a magic act, I would most likely be a true believer and not an Agnostic. But, I haven't and relying on biblical accounts leaves me not knowing beyond a shadow of a doubt, one way or the other, if any actually took place.

As a retired FBI Special Agent, I spent a lot of time in courts where even a single layer of hearsay testimony was routinely disallowed. Rule 802 of the Federal Rules of Evidence dictates hearsay testimony evidence is inadmissible as proof because of the unavailability of cross-examination to test the accuracy of the testimony.

The incalculable levels of hearsay for biblical accounts therefore hold little sway for me. With no way to evaluate the credibility of someone who claimed to have personally observed such miracles, any hope of confirming the truth is essentially unachievable.

Believers need to be willing to acknowledge they don't know for sure if the New Testament accounts are accurate any more than I don't know for sure they aren't.

What has bothered me for a long time is the limited exposure of the alleged miracles performed by Jesus. What's the logic of restricting them to such a relatively small audience over 2 thousand years ago? Why not have similar miracles performed now where modern communications could share them with a large segment of the 7.9 billion?

If Jesus couldn't return to perform them in person, how about the prophets he has allegedly designated as his currently sanctioned earthly representatives? One simple walk on water would definitely get my attention. No need for 37 miracles; even just a single undisputable one would do.

If providing miracles was required to help confirm God's hand over two thousand years ago, why not the same today. Why be required to trust the now unprovable testimony of alleged witnesses so long ago?

Why would an allegedly divinely-inspired plan of salvation by a perfect plan maker, including miracles as indisputable evidence of a godly connection, confine that proof to such a limited audience so long ago? It makes no sense.

That's one reason I remain an Agnostic at the present time.

ELEVEN

THE RESURRECTION

For those professing belief in the Bible, it appears many haven't read it concerning the topic of the resurrection. I say that because of what believers talk about following the death of a loved one. They convey the idea those deceased are now in the presence of God in Heaven having reunited for all eternity with family members and friends who have preceded them in death.

The Bible predicts no such thing; at least, in any kind of resurrected state. The Bible indicates the resurrection will not commence until much later pending the return of Christ to earth. In **1 Thessalonians 4:16**, for example, it states "For the Lord himself shall descend from heaven with a shout, with the voice of the archangel and with the trump of God and the dead in Christ shall rise first." Then, subsequently, a second resurrection will occur after the 1000-year reign (the Millennium) of Christ on the earth.

What then happens to deceased bodies pending their resurrection. Biblical scriptures aren't clear on exactly what happens next. One school of thought is that rotting bodies remain in the grave while their souls sleep in a kind of suspended animation unaware of the passing of time. That sleep comes to an end with the resurrection when the souls are reunited with newly resurrected bodies. If true, that means no immediate reuniting with previously deceased family and friends.

Some scriptures indicate an intermediate conscious state in a paradisical abode. No mention about reuniting with family and friends while awaiting the final judgment day. No description about exactly the physical/spiritual form to be involved.

Neither the conscious or unconscious state make much sense to me. Why waste all that time? What possible justification could there be for putting off the resurrection for such a lengthy period. Why not be judged and resurrected immediately following mortal death? The game plan doesn't seem to depict the involvement of a perfect and compassionate godly planner.

Slightly off topic, a question unanswered in the Bible that should be, is exactly what form a resurrected body would look like. Is it an exact replicate of the body you died with or some perfected version? If you weighed over 400 pounds and couldn't get out of bed, will the resurrected version remain that way for the rest of eternity? Will the ugly remain that way? If perfected, will family and friends even be able to recognize you.

Renowned researchers, probing outside the scope of the Bible, have different takes of what happened to Jesus following his crucifixion and they have nothing to do with him dying on the cross and rising from the dead. Such conjecture deserves to be considered along with what the Bible contends.

One such respected scholar is Barbara Thiering who penned the book, *Jesus the Man*. I picked her because of her expertise in searching ancient records other than the Bible including the Dead Sea Scrolls. Without going into all the convoluted findings and sources of her research (you'll have to read the book), she concluded the following:

(1) Jesus didn't die on the cross. He was fed snake poison mixed with wine while on the cross to avoid the intolerable pain. That rendered him unconscious, but not yet dead. He was removed and transported to a nearby cave site where faithful Jews were waiting in preparation for burial. Although thought to be dead, it was discovered by his followers he wasn't and he was revived by a snake poison antidote made up of the aloe plant causing expulsion of the toxin.

(2) Subsequent sightings of Jesus and conversation with him as reported in the New Testament were, therefore, not with a resurrected being, but with a human being who had never actually died.

(3) Research has allegedly determined Jesus most likely lived past his 70th birthday. He married Mary Magdalene and they had a daughter and son who was also given the name of Jesus and the title of Justus the Righteous One.

(4) Paul's reported meeting with a resurrected Jesus on the road to Damascus, if there was one, was actually a meeting with the still fully human Jesus.

(5) Jesus remained cloistered, to avoid further attempts on this life, for much of the time during the several years after his failed crucifixion He later became more of a public figure in helping to spread his interpretation of how the new and improved Judaism should be lived.

(6) Jesus's final base of operation was most likely in Rome, although there are some legends that he ended up on a Herodian estate in the south of France.

I have no opinion, one way or the other, if Thiering's research reflects the truth. I will say this. As wild as her claims seem to be, I find them just, if not more, believable than the idea of the resurrection promoted in the Bible.

∂ $\oplus$

TWELVE

∂ $\oplus$

FINAL JUDGEMENT

The Bible is replete with scriptures describing a final judgment of all humans following their resurrection. The following scripture sets the tone for the rest:

Revelation 20:11-15: "Then I saw a great white throne and him who was seated on it. From his presence earth and sky fled away, and no place was found for them. And I saw the dead, great and small, standing before the throne, and books were opened. Then another book was opened, which is the book of life. And the dead were judged by what was written in the books, according to what they had done. And the sea gave up the dead who were in it, Death and Hades gave up the dead who were in them, and they were judged, each one of them, according to what they had done. Then Death and Hades were thrown into the lake of fire. This is the second death, the lake of fire. And if anyone's name was not found written in the book of life, he was thrown into the lake of fire."

If there is no final judgement resulting in the quality of post-mortal life, that basic doctrine promulgated by the majority of biblical-oriented organized religions flies out the window. All other doctrinal claims then become open to doubt and reassessment.

I contend my analysis of a pearly gate deception has come up with a reasoned singular argument that can't be credibly countered by popes, prophets, or any of the most prestigious and respected pro-biblical authorities.

My argument doesn't depend on evaluating the authenticity of what has been claimed in millenniums past. It eliminates the argument promoting faith as a way to support the biblical assertions. My proof is now and always has been impervious to any reasonable attempt at repudiation.

The proof of my claim is so obvious and easy to comprehend, it's incomprehensible why it hasn't been broadly brought to light already. But, it hasn't. How could this have been so university ignored? It just doesn't make sense why I'm the only one of the very few, if there have been any others, to argue this all-too-obvious total rejection of any possibility of a final judgment.

The reasoning is so simple. Even if God exists and life after death becomes a reality, an alleged supreme being, touted throughout the Bible as being perfect, loving and compassionate, would never pronounce eternal judgement on how humans conduct their mortal lives. Why? Because a fair and equitable judgement would require all judged be adjudicated based on the exact same standards. A mortal non-starter to say the least.

Organized religion, based in large part on the Bible, can and has made a list of all the offenses determining the quality of one's future eternal existence. That, however, proves useless unless all those judged are tested under identical circumstances.

I've written a book entitled *Pearly Gates Inquiry* detailing eight of the most prevalent reasons why such fair testing hasn't in the past and never will in the future take place. That, because of the reality associated with our mortal existence, the events surrounding each individual life are totally unique. (Anyone interested can locate my book at Barns and Noble or Amazon.) Because this is only a blog and not a book, I'll limit my discussion herein to a brief summary of just one of those reasons. Hopefully, that will prove sufficient to indicate a final judgment is an unattainable fiction.

The life experience of humans is somewhat similar in many ways but radically different in even more. For example, the socioeconomic climate varies dramatically for those who find themselves inhabiting anywhere from the worst off to the best of living environs.

For example, dealing illegal drugs and engaging in other criminal activities proliferate in minority ghettos dominated by gangs who often insist on joining in their illicit activities or suffering dire consequences. So how do you fairly judge someone living in that kind of threatening environment with those lucky enough to be raised in a higher economic setting where such threats are essentially non-existent.

A fair and equitable judgement requires being judged under the same surroundings. Otherwise, the test is a farce and relegation to Heaven or Hell becomes based on an unequal opportunity to flourish or not for the rest of eternity.

The same irrefutable logic applies to other individual circumstances like age, physical/mental limitations, religious indoctrination, IQ, and free agency. A perfect and kindhearted God would realistically establish a judgment bar only if any such resulting verdict was based on an even playing field, the same for all being so adjudicated.

No long back and forth debate required. Life simply doesn't work that way. A fair final judgement is a simple easy-to-understand impossibility.

THIRTEEN

GODLY CONTACT

The Bible is full of contacts between humans and godly beings. As an Agnostic, I would seriously consider becoming one of the most ardent followers to sign up with any organized religion that could prove to me, beyond a reasonable doubt, its founding leader had been in direct contact with a heavenly being intent on establishing a religious following on earth.

I have to believe most any sane person would seriously have to consider joining a religion like that. The fact is untold billions of believers, convinced their particular founder has met that very criterion, have been successfully recruited. If any of them have been correct in their assessment, I may rue the day I decided that agnosticism became my religious belief of choice.

Although far from a comprehensive selection, I'll reflect on three religious leaders I'm somewhat familiar with;

groundbreakers, founding organized religions claiming direct super-natural contact. The Christian, Muslim and Mormon faiths were established by Paul, Mohammed and Joseph Smith respectively. All three replicating the extensive biblical accounts of similar extra-Terrestrial contacts.

I include the Muslim religion in a discussion about the Bible because it teaches that God sent divine revelation through a series of prophets mentioned in the Old Testament including Abraham, Moses and David. However, Muslim scholars also consider the Old Testament to be untrustworthy, inasmuch as it contains corrupted versions of texts that are now lost.

Why did I pick Paul instead of Jesus as the founder of Christianity? That's because he was. Jesus was never anything but a devout Jew, but that's not part of the discussion for this chapter.

The obvious dilemma right off the bat, since the claims have resulted in diametrically contrasting dogma, is at least two of the three must logically be considered bogus. They can't all be true. Whether any of them can furnish credible evidence to validate their extra-terrestrial claims is open to serious skepticism.

At any rate, all three made claims similarly miraculous. All three claimed direct contact with heavenly beings; Paul with a resurrected Jesus; Mohammed with the angel Gabriel; and Joseph Smith with both a resurrected Jesus and God the Father. Instead of attempting to create new godly beings, all three claimed contacts with biblical heavenly personages already accepted by most potential converts; thus, making it easier to enlist prospective converts.

Convincing me faith proves, beyond a shadow of a doubt, a particular religious organization is the authentic one is unpersuasive. Member faith in all three denominations is similarly strident.

So, what do we end up with? As already noted, at least two of my selections had to have been making fraudulent or mentally-flawed claims. There is, in fact, insufficient collaborative evidence to support the claims of any of the three. None of the miraculous assertions could withstand scrutiny today in a court of law.

Present me with irrefutable proof that wouldn't be thrown out of court as unreliable hearsay. Evidence based on unbiased witnesses who could withstand stringent cross-examination, Then, and only then, I might seriously be willing to consider changing my Agnostic persona to that of a true believer.

FOURTEEN

FAITH

I have addressed the topic of faith in one way or another in several of the books I've published so far. It seems every time I talk to someone about my Agnostic tendencies relating to the tenants of organized religion, the concept of faith ends up being a primary element of whatever is being discussed.

This has been especially the case when having discussions concerning the credibility of the Bible. Just as I think I've made a logical case for my doubt, the faith card comes into play and any further attempt to convince from my point of view is a waste of time.

And yet, just as I conclude blind faith is the worst thing ever, somebody tells me a personal experience or the experience of someone else that causes me to rethink my misgiving. The purpose of this chapter is to briefly look a little deeper into the pros and cons of faith and its effect on the human race.

Webster defines faith as "unquestioning belief that doesn't require proof or evidence." That's the definition I'm referring to herein. Absolute belief in the Bible is an example of the kind of problematic faith that can't be proven beyond a reasonable doubt even though those holding such views often have no uncertainty whatsoever about its claimed absolute veracity.

Does faith improve an individual's life or the lives of those around that person even if doesn't help prove the authenticity of the Bible? That's the question an Agnostic like myself is ultimately forced to seriously consider. Does the truth really matter if the quality of life is improved as a result? On the other hand, what are the dangerous perils such faith can foreshadow?

Those critical of the negative power of faith often point to the evil that resulted from the Christian Inquisitions when hundreds of thousands of blameless victims were tortured and killed for not adhering to Christian biblical doctrine. Established around the 12th century, the Inquisition consisted of a general religious tribunal established for the discovery and suppression of heresy.

Historians distinguish four different manifestations of the Inquisition including the Medieval Inquisition (1184-1230s), the Spanish Inquisition (1478-1834), the Portuguese Inquisition (1536-1821), and the Roman Inquisition (1542-1860). I won't take time here to detail the unbelievable inhumanity that resulted from those who were convinced that their religious faith somehow authorized them to excruciate and annihilate those who didn't meet their doctrinal standards. That sad record is easily researchable for all to sadly comprehend.

More current examples of the perils of blind faith are evident among the devout followers of the Branch Davidians, Heaven's Gate and the People's Temple. It's clear the Christian faith that members displayed in all these instances was not only based on apparently false religious doctrine, but caused unconscionable grief and death in the process.

On the opposite end of the spectrum, the positive power of faith can be found in many biblically- oriented denominations and organizations today that concentrate on building positive character traits and helping those in need. Alcohol and drug treatment programs are good examples where faith in the Bible and prayer are often critical elements in helping addicts come clean.

The convict who has been sentenced to life in prison, subsequently accepting Jesus as Lord and Savior, typifies the benefit of faith, blind or not. Not only is such a convert potentially less dangerous to fellow inmates, but the remainder of his or her life may end up more purposeful and less hopeless because of the biblical concept of repentance and eternal salvation.

I'm aware of numerous instances where the leaders of various Christian denominations are less interested in proving the veracity of what the Bible has to say, and more involved with improving the lives of its members and helping the needy. Although still preaching the existence of a loving Christian God, they don't place a great emphasis on the infallibility of their founding doctrine. For example, they spend less time on trying to disprove evolution because of the story of the creation in the book of Genesis, and more time in inspiring practical ways to build strong family ties and avoid self-destructive behavior.

Back to the bad. In his book, *The End of Faith (p. 26),* Sam Harris chronicles the destructive side of fervent faith including "The recent conflicts in Palestine (Jews v. Muslims), The Balkans (Orthodox Serbians v. Catholic Croatians; Orthodox Serbians v. Bosnian and Albanian

Muslims), Northern Ireland (Protestants v. Catholics), Kashmir (Muslims v. Hindus), Sudan (Muslims v. Christians and Animists), Nigeria (Muslims v. Christians), Ethiopia and Eritrea (Muslims v. Christians), Sri Lanka (Sinhalese Buddhists v. Tamil Hindus), Indonesia (Muslims v. Timorese Christians), and the Caucasus (Orthodox Russians v. Chechen Muslims; Muslim Azerbaijanis v. Catholic and Orthodox Armenians)..."

Harris points to what he contends could end up being the most tragic result of misplaced faith in the history of the world. His concern centers on Muslim extremism in combination with the escalating threat of nuclear annihilation.

Unlike the cold war between the United States and Russia where neither side wanted to risk their own devastation, Muslim terrorists, should they gain control of nuclear weaponry, appear to have no compulsion to prevent their own self-destruction in order to destroy their enemies. This glorification of dying and going to heaven to obtain unimaginable glory and reward for fighting infidels changes the whole concept of mutual nuclear deterrence.

Hopefully, by now, you've begun to see the problem of trying to define blind faith as resulting in either bad or good. It seems it can go either way depending on how it is applied. If it helps believers live a better life and assist others in need, it's hard not to agree it promotes mostly good.

One common denominator that appears to make faith turn bad is when charismatic zealots, touting bogus religious dogma, attempt to impose their twisted interpretation of faith on others. Whether that imposition takes the form of a governmental theocracy or the attempt to religiously dominate a democracy, it seems that trouble is not far away.

My intention then is to respect and even encourage, in selected instances, the kinds of blind biblical faith improving the lives of its members regardless of whether being founded on truth and reason.

At the same time, I will remain highly suspicious and vigilant against those whose warped faith can't seem to stop them from attempting to impose the same on others; particularly, those who are mentally/emotionally unstable and thus especially prone to destructive charismatic manipulation.

FIFTEEN

DEATH'S TREPIDATION

A fellow Agnostic made an off-the-cuff comment to me a while back taking me by surprise. He said he kind of missed the time as a former fully-committed Christian when he had faith in the Bible assuring him of a heavenly after-life following his earthly demise.

He explained his former faithful ignorance resulted in a sort of peaceful bliss and reassurance that no longer exists. That seemed sad to me. Sad, in that it doesn't seem right that confronting the truth about the Bible's fallibility might adversely upend a person's mortal sense of happiness and security.

I'm presently unsure if a supreme being exists or life after death is a realistic likelihood. There're other potential creationist scenarios. For example, as previously mentioned, the existence of an extraterrestrial grand designer who's been responsible for humanity, but never intended any of us make it past mortality.

What I'm convinced of is organized religion dependance on the Bible can't prove how humans originated; any more than the alleged validity of the other super-natural events found in the Bible Certainty, no convincing evidence guaranteeing resurrection after death.

I appreciate my friend's discomfort over his loss of his previous guarantee of an eternal existence. For example, when we lose loved ones, it's almost unthinkable to even consider the possibility we may never see them again.

Still, even though not experiencing any confident tranquility of life after death, my present state of mind is relaxed; now accepting my Agnostic philosophy of not knowing, one way or the other, about the reality of a supreme being or if life after death exists. Hoping immortality comes to fruition, but not expecting it out of any sense of inevitability.

I instead try to concentrate on living, as far as possible, a happy and fulfilling mortal life uninhibited by worrying what may or may not happen after it's over. As far as being overly anxious about mortal death being the end of me, I'm not.

If there's more after I die, that will be a wonderful outcome. If not, I'm going to cease to exist and obviously won't experience any future remorse. Fixating about the existence of a God or an afterlife isn't worth wasting time distressing about.

My respectful recommendation: Live within the law and employ a moral compass. Enjoy life without the unreasonable inhibitions demanded by organized religion. Don't let unprovable biblical claims about what happens after death cause undue stress.

SIXTEEN

FINAL THOUGHTS

It continues to astound me when I keep running into believers who claim every word in the Bible is true and represents the flawless resolve of its God. Questioning if they've read and studied the Bible, I usually determine they haven't in any meaningful way. Still, they claim their faith in its infallibility is unassailable. Again and again, I find it hard to debate with someone whose lack of knowledge is replaced by belief that can't be supported by fact or common sense.

This book is brief when considering the plethora of additional troubling biblical possibilities. I determined the few I established herein are sufficient to make the point. I've seen no reason in going on and on with more of the same. If the doubts I've set forth don't establish that the Bible can't be trusted, adding more wouldn't likely make a difference.

My negative critique usually focuses first on the absurdity contained in the Old Testament (OT). I point out numerous passages starting with Genesis. Advocates seem somewhat flummoxed when they can't intelligently respond to the foolish account of the creation going against every fundamental principle known to science. It's like they've never before made the effort to carefully read and seriously ponder such foolish assertions.

I can feel their consternation building when, for possibly the first time, they begin to realize the dark side of their God in the next books of Exodus and Leviticus; where, He is again and again depicted to be a maniacal vengeful egotist with no concern shown for innocent human life.

It's obvious this wasn't the same God they were taught about in Sunday School. I can tell they're starting to think of some kind of justification why this part of the Bible doesn't appear to represent the loving and compassionate deity they have come to worship so devoutly.

I know my conversation with those who claim biblical perfection are in for a rough ride when we start to consider the imperfect content in the New Testament (NT). At that point, I usually let them off the hook in trying to defend the OT. I let them know the only thing they have to concern themselves with is showing me why everything in the NT represents the whole truth and nothing but. It's usually the beginning of the end of a credible response with the concept of unquestioning faith creeping onto center stage.

Bart D. Ehrman, author of *Jesus Interrupted,* suggests the best way to test the numerous contradictions in the NT is to establish a horizontal rather than vertical analysis of the same biblical events and teachings. That was the method I used in chapter 7. Vertical is where the books and chapters are read independently. Horizontal requires taking the same events discussed in different part of the NT and placing them side by side to discover any inconsistencies.

As I previous noted, contradicting accounts of the same events can all be false, but they can't be all true. Discovering discrepancy after discrepancy needs to be viewed as seriously undercutting the reliability of the NT as a whole.

I've noticed those, who promote the Bible, tend to pick and choose excerpts that validate the best it has to offer. They tend to ignore the parts that don't meet that standard. Actually, most haven't even read enough of the Bible to uncover those parts that should leave them doubting any godly input of its composition.

As I've tried to make clear, what may bother me the most, about the content of the Bible, is that all the miracles and godly involvement happened so long ago. There's no way now to prove what did or didn't take place. That glaring reality, nothing of a similar nature having currently transpired, creates rational suspicion it didn't back then either.

If there was no hesitation to flout the super-natural then, among a relatively trivial audience, why not now with the internet and world-wide potential audience estimated at 7.76 billion.

With nary an angel making a verifiable public appearance today, the former biblical appearances defy any credible proof. Without the hint of a biblical-like miracle now, what sense does it make to so easily accept what happened then? Until events like that transpire in the present, with the evidence irrefutable, my outlook as a doubting Thomas remains unaltered.

Printed in the United States
by Baker & Taylor Publisher Services